A Brief History of the Sewing Machine
Without the boring bits
By
Alex Askaroff

The rights of Alex Askaroff as author
of this work have been asserted by him
in accordance with the Copyright,
Designs and Patents Act 1993.
©

To see Alex Askaroff's work
Visit Amazon

A Brief History of the Sewing Machine

Without the boring bits
By
Alex Askaroff

This is no masterpiece. It's more a self-published labour of love from someone who has spent a lifetime in the sewing trade and a million hours gathering facts for you. From my vast profits of around 10p a book I'll retire to my allotment and grow cabbages. Why write it? Well no one else bothers! Please forgive my spelling, United Kingdom English, and enjoy it in the spirit it was written. Also I found it impossible to split into chapters. Just go with the flow.

"One of the few useful things ever invented"

Mahatma Gandhi

1801

Here it is, eighteen oh one,

Me 'ousework now has all been done.

I'll drag out my piecework, to make a bob,

Sit me down, before the hob.

Turn the chair, to get the light,

Sew what I can, before the night!

Here in the village, there's six of us,

Work needle and thread, our hands all callus!

We get brought the cloth, all cut out, in red,

We connects it all, by pulling thick thread.

The red dye, when the cloth is fresh, mind,

Stains our hands likewise, we find.

We don't get paid much, we all gripes,

But if I don't sew, me 'usband stripes

Me back wiv 'is belt! And , Oh, that 'urts,

I think I'd rather sew some shirts!

'E 'as no bleedin' pity in 'im, see?

Drinks all the money earned by me!

© Rob Van De Laak

Who invented the sewing machine? People are always asking me. It's a great story. Put the kettle on, make a nice cuppa and read all about it. I will take you on a brief and interesting history tour of one of the most useful inventions of the 19th Century.

By the middle of the Victorian Era sewing machines were taking hold. Before that period all fabric would have been joined by hand, every single stitch. The method hardly changes since Stone Age times. Clothes were slow and timely to produce and cost a lot of money, even the thread cost a fortune. Factories around the world were employing people (mainly women because they were better at it) to sew all day long. I once heard that a factory in America employed over 3,000 women sewing by hand.

As the population of our planet exploded and the Industrial revolution took hold someone had to come up with a solution of how to join two pieces of fabric quicker and cheaper than by hand. This in turn led to a fascinating trail of invention and failure. Some inventors died in poverty some became richer beyond all their dreams. One man, Isaac Singer, became famous. His name is still one of the most well-known names all over the world.

So how did it all begin? First of all I want you to read a quote from one of the Sewing Machine Pioneers, James Edward Allen Gibbs. James was the son of a Shenandoah farmer born 1 August 1829.

He witnessed the major development of the sewing machine. In 1901 he was interviewed about his inventions and patents. No other person alive was better qualified to quote on the subject.

His words are absolutely crucial in understanding the development of the sewing machine.

"No useful sewing machine was ever invented by one man; and all first attempts to do work by machinery, previously done by hand, have been failures. It is only after several able inventors have failed in attempt, that someone with the mental powers to

combine the efforts of others with his own, at last produces a practicable sewing machine."

James Gibbs

That is the crux of it. Sewing machine manufacture started slowly and was constantly interrupted. However in the 50 years from 1846 the sewing machine went from a circus attraction to a necessity for every household.

The Victorian Era, with its massive expansion in industry and technology proved to be the fertile ground from which the sewing machine grew.

By the year 1900 over 20 million sewing machines a year were being produced from factories all over the world.

It is true to say that, until the mobile phone, no single invention was as eagerly accepted by people in all four corners of the planet as the humble sewing machine.

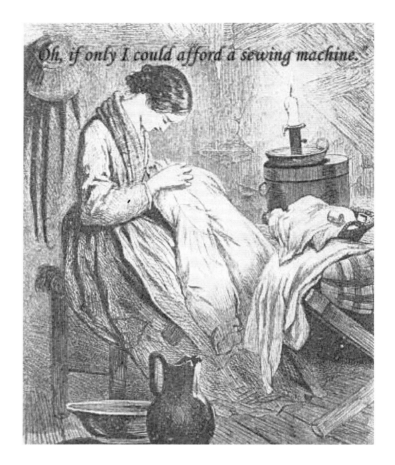

Everyone knew whoever invented a good sewing machine would become rich. Isaac Singer and Elias Howe were two of the first men to become amazingly wealthy from their sewing machines.

Stitch! Stitch! Stitch!

With fingers weary and worn,
With eyelids heavy and red,
A woman sat in unwomanly rags,
Plying her needle and thread

Yet still, with a voice of sweet pitch
Wished its tone could reach the Rich!

For in poverty, hunger and dirt,
She sang the Song of the Shirt

Who actually invented the sewing machine?

Was it the Germans who invented the sewing machine? They think they did. Was it the French? Yep, they know it was them. How about the British! We invented everything. Didn't we? The Chinese? In their 5,000 plus-year history and all that silk, they must have invented it! How about the Egyptians and all their cotton! No hieroglyphics of sewing machines discovered yet!

The truth is many nations can claim that they invented the humble sewing machine, and many do. Read on...

Let's just stop and think for a second. When you next look at the humble sewing machine, wonder how the world would be without it! Here is a quote from the Victorian press. Remember this is a 19th Century quote.

"In the history of the world the sewing machine has freed more women from the drudgery of manual work than any invention to date!"

What we have to do is look at the facts that we know at present. There is no saying that the facts we have today are written in stone and that some Russian won't crawl out of the Siberian wastelands clutching a wood and ivory sewing machine made by great Uncle Ivan.

Even back as early as the Elizabethan Period and later in the time of King Charles I, in the 1640's, people were applying for early patents or royal letters of protection or 'monopolies' for weird and wonderful mechanisms. However we have no firm proof of the machines and as poor old Charlie came a croper we shall never know. In 1649 they removed his head! His hand stitched and blood stained shirt is on display at Longleat.

So we had better go by proven dates.

The first inventor of the sewing machine that we can be sure of was patented in England in 1755. Yes! Come-on-England. Where did I put my flag!

Charles Weisenthal 1755

Charles Weisenthal

One Charles Weisenthal (ok, so he was German, but, he was in England) took out a patent for a needle to be used for mechanical sewing. Unfortunately, what sort of mechanical sewing we do not know for a description of the machine was not properly mentioned in the patent.

Thomas Saint

Back in England in 1790, Sorry America, Thomas Saint really cracked it. Not only did he patent a sewing machine but he also provided enough plans that a replica could be built. British Patent No. 1764 was awarded to Thomas Saint, a London cabinetmaker.

Due to several other patents dealing with leather and products to treat leather, the patent was filed under "Glues & Varnishes" and was not discovered until 1873/4 when the British sewing machine pioneer Newton Wilson was researching his history of the sewing machine. He stumbled upon Thomas Saint's chain stitch machine and was amazed. He actually built a working model using Saint's patent drawings and a few modifications.

An early 1860 woodcut of the Newton Wilson Family sewing machine. It was Newton Wilson who discovered Thomas Saint's misfiled patent.

Though the exact replica of Saint's machine **did not sew,** people often patent things with great urgency to protect their inventions. Also patents are rarely the exact final product that comes onto the market. In the case of Thomas Saint a few minor modifications were made to his machine and it sewed like a dream. There is no doubt he would have made these modifications.

Note the case of Elijah Grey! He should be a household name but I bet you have never heard of him? Let me tell you why. Elijah was beaten to the patent office **by a few hours** by Alexander Graham Bell. Bell went on to patent the talking wire. Elijah went home in tears (probably) and faded into oblivion.

In fact recent discoveries have shown that many people actually filed slightly altered patents to stop industrial espionage. This still goes on today.

Copies of patents were valuable and often sold to the highest bidder.

Saint may have even deliberately filed a patent that he knew would not work to protect his main ideas while he perfected his machine!

A Thomas Saint replica

So now we know that Saint's patent needed some modification to sew, but I have no doubt he would have performed the modifications if he could have so, we must give him brownie points for effort, though no points for giving up early. Perhaps he had an urgent cabinet to finish!

The modified replica above does sew! Mind you weird looking or what! Can't see that catching on in a hurry. It looks more like some printing press or medieval instrument of torture.

But I have to say, yeehaaa... Another first for England, along with cricket, golf, rugby, soccer, snooker and my favourite, afternoon tea, promptly at four, with cucumber and salmon sandwiches of course!

The British still claim to have invented the sewing machine!

Thomas Stone

In 1804 we go to France where Thomas Stone, (not a particularly French name) had patented a machine that we know nothing about...Yet!

That must have been a good year as we have two other gentlemen on the scene, a James Henderson and a canny Scot, and Mr Duncan, for an embroidery machine. Again, nothing has come to light about their machines but we live in hope.

Baltasar Krems

Baltasar Krem's hat making machine

Balthasar Krems was born on November 27th 1760 in Mayen, Rhineland and died at the age of 53 on May 4th 1813 in the same town.

Balthasar Krems used to make cardigans and caps, also Phrygian caps (like the ones worn during the French revolution). Mayen was occupied by French troops from 1794 to 1815. With lots of orders, around 1810, he came up with a unique sewing machine which he used to sew the seams of his caps.

Some say that Balthasar invented the sewing machine needle with the eye at the pointed end. Something that a few other inventors, including Elias Howe, would dispute. Balthasar's sewing machine was pedal operated and sewed a continuous-circular chain stitch with a basic wheel feed mechanism (which he also invented).

The sewing needle pricked horizontally through the fabric and formed the first loop, then a hook caught the loop and held it until the needle came back with the next thread, thus forming the chain-stitch. It was basic but it worked faster than sewing by hand.

There is a bust of Balthasar Krems in Mayen on the Genoveva castle wall. There is also one of his type of machines at the Eifel museum in Mayen and another replica at the Deutsche Museum in Munich.

Because old Balt did not patent his design we cannot be sure of the exact dates or his exact designs, but we do know he was German, yavol!

The Germans still claim to have invented the sewing machine!

Josef Madersperger 1768-1850

Josef Madersperger died a pauper in a Vienna poorhouse

Now, across the border to the land of sachertorte, lederhosen and schnitzel, you guessed it, Austria.

The year is 1814, Napoleon is about to meet his Waterloo and Josef Madersperger, a humble tailor is building the first of several sewing machines.

Although he had been working on his machine since 1807 it was not until 1815 that he was granted patent rights on his model.

He had tried in vain for years to get his machine right and in 1839 he almost cracked it. In 1841 his machine was awarded a bronze medal but he could not find a manufacturer to take it on.

Josef had invested every penny in his invention and spent his whole life working on it. However he was still making the same old mistake trying to make his machines copy the hand movement of sewing girls.

Josef's ill-fated and highly complex machine

Eventually Josef gave his model away and a few years later, in 1850, he died a pauper in the poor house in Vienna. In 1950 Austria celebrated his inventive genius with a series of stamps for their post and they even have a statue of him.

The Austrians still claim to have invented the sewing machine!

Hold on I hear you shouting! What about America! Well at last, we come to the land of the free and the home of the brave.

John Knowles
&
John Adams Doge

In 1818 John Knowles and his partner, John Adams Doge, made a sewing machine. It really stitches! But there is a catch! Isn't there always! The machine will only stitch a few inches of cloth before the cloth has to be taken out and reset. What a waste of time. Much faster to still carry on hand sewing, so chuck that in the bin!

At this rate it looks as if no one is going to figure out the first piece of engineering to enter the domestic household. But we have not finished, the wheels of the industrial revolution are turning and great minds are at work.

Henry Lye

In 1826, Henry Lye of Philadelphia, PA, patented a sewing machine of sorts but fire destroyed the patent office and his invention. Don't worry there is more fire coming up!

We now skip back over the ocean to France, home of frog's legs, brie and snail snacks. I bet their buffets are fun!

Now things are really going to heat up for we have a real invention that actually works. It may interest you to know that as I write Ray Rushton from the London Sewing Machine Museum has acquired a genuine Thimonnier sewing machine. It was reputed to have cost him a king's ransom.

Barthelemy Thimonnier

Around 1829-30 the first real sewing machine that we know of was born. Barthelemy Thimonnier (I'm going to call him Bart now as it makes my head hurt spelling his name) took out a patent for a barbed needled to be used in his **sewing machine**.

Bart's wooden machine was not a hit with the French tailors. Well, they liked to hit it but not sew with it!

The machine, made of wood, actually worked, producing a chain stitch or tambour stitch, you know the sort of stitch you find across potato sacks. In fact it worked so well that he gained a contract to build loads of them. They were used to sew uniforms for the French army.

Here is his American patent application many years later.

United States Patent Office
Patent 7622 September 3 1850

Be it known that I, Barthélemy Thimonnier, Aine, of Amplepuis, Department of Du Rhone, in the Republic of France, a citizen of France. Have invented or discovered new and useful improvement to the sewing machine for the forming of stitches in fabrics.

Before long Bart was sewing away with dozens of machines taking work from the hungry tailors of Paris. We all know what Frenchmen are like when their blood is up. Madame Guillotine was still warm from their revolution. In 1831 it all came to a head at his workshop in Rue de Sevres where 80 of his wooden machines were busily sewing away.

The angry tailors, now out of work because of the modern machines, gathered outside Bart's premises and then stormed in.

At first they threw garlic at the machines but to their amazement they bounced off!

They decided to have a booze up and torch Bart's workshop. The crowd watched as poor old Bart headed for the hills, his business in flames.

Bart, unperturbed and with that usual French resilience, started all over again with an even better model.

Nevertheless, those sneaky tailors knew what he was up to and set about the poor fellow, this time with far more powerful weapons, strings of onions!

Barthelemy Thimonnier

Bart fled to England just like the many aristocrats that had feared for their lives during the French Revolution years earlier. Where was the Scarlet Pimpernel when he was needed eh!

Bart flogged his patents to a company in Manchester but never regained his former success and although he had made the first reasonable sewing machine it did not stop the poor old tailor ending up like his Austrian counterpart. Poor old Bart died in poverty in Amplepuis on the 5th of August 1857.

We have to step back a little and ask ourselves why so many workmen were afraid of machines!

Well it all boiled down to jobs. They had no idea that the industry they were destroying would actually end up employing untold numbers of workers across the globe. The fact is, like many of us today, they feared change.

To make things worse for poor old Bart he probably witnessed the birth of the real sewing machine industry as when he died in 1857 many of the major inventors had produced practical sewing machines and made loads of dosh from them. Talk about lemon juice on a paper cut!

The French still claim to have invented the sewing machine!

However, we are jumping ahead. I do hope you are enjoying the history so far, crazy isn't it!

Newton and Archibold

In 1841 Newton and Archibold, in England, designed a chain-stitch machine employing an eye-pointed needle, little else is known of their invention. No fun there, I am missing those French tailors already! So where do we go now, Japan, no, India...Could be! No, we are off to America, la-la-la-laaa-America. Where's my hotdog and mayo!

John James Greenough

The John James Greenough machine of 1842

In 1842 John James Greenough, patented a sewing machine with a stitch forming mechanism. It had a device for presenting work onto a double pointed needle with an eye in the middle! How weird is that! I bet he pricked his fingers a few times!

Frank Goulding

In 1843, Dr Frank Goulding of Macon, Georgia, also created a sewing device but once again he failed to develop it, as did Walter Hunt. You'll read a little about him later. He also he has his own book in my Sewing Machine Pioneer Series.

What a lot of failures we have in our story! No wonder no one trusted Singer's invention when he tried to sell it...Oop's now I given the story away!

The problem is that no one has yet invented a machine that was much good and they all looked like medieval torture instruments. The big mistake was trying to copy the human hand movements that made a stitch. That was until Walter Hunt came along.

We are getting close to the real inventors so stay with us. As I mentioned, Walter has his own great story in my Sewing Machine Pioneer Series.

Walter Hunt

With Walter, for the first time, we see a machine that we can recognise as a sewing machine. One that can be sold to every household.

Things are looking, up especially in America where the inventor of the Safety Pin was hard at work.

Walter Hunt is in his basement. He is arguing with his daughter. Walter has made a sewing machine that produces a lockstitch. What is more it is not the old fangled type that tried to copy the movements of the human hand. It is a brand new design that really works. It even had two spools of thread. The year was 1834.

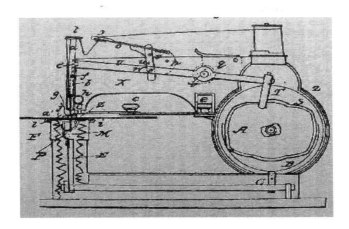

His machine took two spools of thread and a needle that looks similar to the ones we use today. It produces a lockstitch. Its only drawback was short seams. Look on the positive side, it would have been great for dolls clothes!

Walter's daughter is giving him an ear bashing in the basement. Does he not realise how many women will be put out of work if he patents his **sewing monster**! People will starve in the streets!

Eventually Walter gives in and leaves his invention to gather dust. Little did he realise that firstly, he would actually create endless jobs for workers as sewing machines made clothes cheaper and more available to the masses. But he would also have become rich in the process. Then he would have been able to send his aggravating daughter to Swiss finishing school.

Walter Hunt was a prolific inventor and must have had mixed feeling about people because he also invented a repeating rifle!

Still, Walter disappears from our story. He does reappear patenting an improved model of his earlier invention in 1854 (some 20 years after he first developed it) but it is all way too late by then. He also appeared in many court cases between several of the larger sewing machine characters all bluffing their way through court, but that's a long way off. If you read my history on Isaac Singer you can see what part he played and the devious tricks Isaac got up to.

Walter Hunt will always be remembered not for the sewing machine but for another point in history. He invented the safety pin! See what I did there!

Mind you, he also invented a sort of *cure all* life preserver tonic. Probably early Wild West snake oil. Best forget about that. So let us finish with this colourful character and get back to business.

John Fisher

In 1844, back in England, John Fisher patented a lace-making machine that sewed. However, the patent was misfiled and John did not pursue his invention.

Now, at last, I hear some cry, we come to one of the most important dates, and people, in sewing history.

Elias Howe

The year 1844 was a good year for in America a young farmer was about to shake the sewing world.

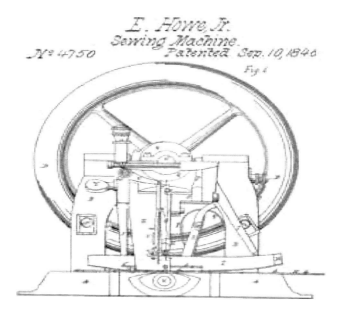

Howe's 1846 patent. It does not look much like a sewing machine!

Elias Howe finished his machine around 1844 or 1845 and patented it in 1846. A Massachusetts farmer, Elias went on to become one of the richest men in the world. However shortly after his death his wealth disappeared as quickly as snow in summer. His amazing life story is in another of my Sewing Machine Pioneer Series.

Elias tried in vain to sell his contraption, it had no takers in America. The poor farmer had spent months perfecting a machine that once again basically copied the sweeping hand movement. However he had several good ideas that were similar to Hunt's. Clever Elias took the precaution of patenting them.

He travelled to England where his brother, Amasa, had found a possible purchaser and backer. All this ended in tears and a disappointment. Broke, Elias headed home.

On arriving back in America he found things had changed. Much like the computer industry today, a year can be a long time with new developments taking place almost weekly.

Elias found that in his absence, sewing machines had hit the big time. Dozens of sewing machine companies had sprung up and many of them were using his patents! Especially his clever needle with the long groove and the hole at the point end and his brilliant small metal shuttle!

Elias understandably went ballistic, suing everyone he could, including our most famous sewing machine entrepreneur, Isaac Singer.

In 1850 Isaac had won a bet, so he says, to make a better sewing machine than what was available on the market.

It was patented in 1851 and changed our world, well our clothes anyway.

The first reliable sewing machine with a guarantee had arrived. This one invention made Isaac amazingly wealthy and boy did he spend it! Unfortunately he had one big fly in his ointment and that was Elias Howe.

Elias Howe was poor at selling his sewing machine but brill in court he must have had good lawyers. He made a fortune. He made two fortunes, not from producing sewing machines but from suing everyone that did.

In addition, those he did not sue he charged a ridiculous licence fee, just like the BBC does to us here in Britain to watch TV.

The Sewing Machine Cartel

Eventually, Elias and the other big boys in the sewing industry got fed up with fighting and got together. They formed the Sewing Machine Cartel. Then they fought everyone else. What fun!

It was totally illegal and it was brought to an end years later by a change in the law. However they all made a mint out of it while it lasted.

Howe then went on to have a rather dubious history of his side of events published. This painted him as the only real inventor of the sewing machine.

A rather far-fetched picture by all accounts. His machine would never have caught on. It could only sew in short straight lengths. Mind you he made a good needle, better than almost anyone at the time, and a brilliant shuttle.

Just for your records or school project the cartel were, Mr Wheeler and Mr Wilson, Isaac Singer, Mr Grover and his partner Mr Baker and of course Elias Howe and a few small fry to keep the paperwork in order.

It was Allen B. Wilson that really helped with his patented method of feeding the work through the machine with a set of teeth. It was called the four-motion-feed and is still used today.

The superb 1860 long arm Grover & Baker

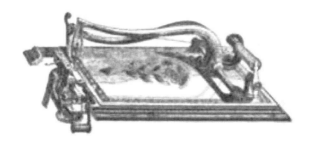

An early Wheeler & Wilson

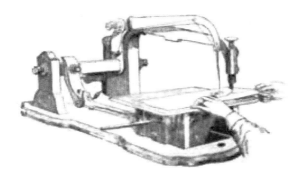

Elias could not have been all bad as he used some of his enormous wealth to equip a whole Union infantry regiment in the American Civil War then enlisted himself, as a private. I loved writing his book in my Sewing Machine Pioneer Series (a No1 New Release).

Out of all these manufacturers, by 1851 Isaac Singer had the best machine. It incorporated many features that we still see today. He really won hands down with his treadle which allowed both hands free for sewing.

Although Isaac cannot be credited with any major invention, (he allegedly copied just about everything) he did make a blinder of a sewing machine and had a few patents to boot. You just have to read my story on him, loads of scandals. It's better than any soap opera.

Of course the answer was there in front of us all the time. Isaac's machine bears a startling resemblance to the gearing and shafts on water mills that had been grinding flour for over 2,000 years!

His genius lay in copying and then improving on what was around at the time. Was there a little bit of Japanese blood in him?

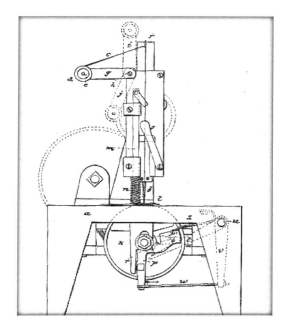

Isaac Singer's 1851 model A. Lots of cogs and gears. It fed the work with a revolving wheel.

Basically, the human mind rarely makes huge leaps in technology. In fact I think it is just about impossible. If it was we would have evolved much faster than we did.

I think people see an idea and improve on it. Which, I believe, is what happened with the sewing machine.

The perfect example is James Edward Allen Gibb. He saw a picture of a sewing machine, the top half, and went to work. He made a perfect sewing machine. Unable to see the bottom half he invented an entirely new method of stitching. What we ended up with was the stunning Wilcox & Gibbs Chain stitch machine.

Just one more before it all gets way too messy.

Charles Judkins

In 1851 C T Judkins was already exhibiting and selling his weird box-shaped sewing machines.

At the Great Exhibition in 1851 Charles Judkins demonstrated his power driven machine by sewing nearly 500 stitches into fabric in one minute.

As a point of note his was the only British sewing machine exhibited. How that changed in a few short years. The world was ready for the sewing machine.

The most useful invention of the Victorian era

From the early 1850's, the handful of inventors (who I call the sewing machine pioneers) turned, firstly into hundreds and then to thousands. From now on no one can keep track.

The Singer Company went on to perfect the sewing machine and dominated world production for the next century. I have a great little booklet about the rise and fall of Singer manufacturing in Britain that explains a little of how the great company came and went.

To begin with the press were not very positive about sewing machines. However they soon caught on as sewing factories bloomed.

The general impression has sprung up that the invention on the whole is a failure.
Illustrated London News 1854

This is the Somervell Brothers clothing and coat factory in Netherfield, Kendal, 1862. It shows that after a few hiccups with the new-fangled sewing machines they caught on. In a few short years mechanisation of clothes had quickly taken hold. Manufacturing times dropped, priced dropped and the high street retailer was born!

The first mass produced domestic appliance in history had arrived in the household. However it was not as simple as you may think.

The first reliable sewing machines were here at last. However, because everyone had been plagued by countless poor and faulty machines before, no one trusted these new ones. Once the factories got their production right, allowed part payments for their machines and gave good guarantees, they were on a roll.

Legend tells that gun makers like Winchester and Samuel Colt toured the sewing machine factories perfecting their mass production techniques for arms.

Many of the factories that had tried the first machines had their fingers burnt and were reluctant to waste more money, especially while labour was so cheap.

Isaac Singer went into overdrive and his early acting skills came into their own as he paraded his machines around like a fairground attraction.

This woodcut illustration from 1854 shows possibly the first factory in Britain to use sewing machines, powered by a steam engine which drove belts below each machine. George Holloway successfully converted his clothing factory to sewing machines using early C T

Judkins of Manchester sewing machines. Twenty sewing machines doing the work of 60 women. The tide was turning...

From our new machines we can produce hundreds of pairs of men's working trousers a week. The days of the poor needlewoman are over.

Slowly, slowly sewing machines started to sell in numbers. 100 turned into a thousand and so on. Surprisingly there was a huge surge in sales during The American Civil War.

By the middle of the 1850's everyone could see the light and from then on it was all down to good marketing. Some, like Singer and Pfaff were marketing experts and their machines flourished. Many, like poor old Josef & Bart mentioned earlier, died in poverty.

By the late Victorian period the sewing machine had been hailed as the most useful invention of the century, releasing women from the drudgery of endless hours of sewing by hand.

Factories sprung up in almost every country in the world to feed the insatiable demand for the sewing machine. Germany had over 300 factories some working 24 hours a day, producing countless numbers of sewing machines.

By 1926 the American patent office had over 150,000 different patent models. Tricky dusting those!

Within decades, millions of sewing machines were being sold to every corner of the world and all our clothes looked much better!

Today, there are some sewing machines that are so advanced they can scan a pattern, duplicate it, then store the pattern in case it is needed again and maintain themselves. In addition (as if that is not enough) some actually speak to you when there is a problem. Boy do they drive me mad when I am fixing them! I often think an aspirin may help!

There is no doubt that Isaac Merritt Singer put together the first marketable sewing machine that was reliable, did what it was designed to do, and came with a guarantee that was worth the paper it was written on.

His machine set the manufacturing world on fire and then spread from the factories to the homes until almost every household had the use of a sewing machine.

It is true to say that no single invention had ever been as eagerly accepted by people in all four corners of the planet as the humble, and often overlooked, sewing machine.

It is one small machine that silently touches our daily lives and I expect that right now every single reader will be able to see something stitched on a sewing machine, even if they are sitting on it!

So there we have it, a brief history of the first sewing machine inventors. Great fun but as clear as mud eh!

Like I said at the beginning, many countries can claim to have given birth to the first sewing machine, but like Elias Howe and Isaac Singer found out, it would be hard to prove in court.

I hope that you have enjoyed my short tale. Not as boring as one might assume m'lord!

The End

In 1882 an electric sewing machine was demonstrated to the public at Crystal Palace, the world of sewing had changed forever.

Isaac Singer
The First capitalist

No1 New Release Amazon 2014. Most of us know the name Singer but few are aware of his amazing life story, his rags to riches journey from a little runaway to one of the richest men of his age. The story of Isaac Merritt Singer will blow your mind, his wives and lovers, castles and palaces.

No1 New Release. No1 Bestseller
Amazon certified.

*If this isn't the perfect book it's close to it!
I'm on my third run though already.
Love it, love it, love it.
F. Watson USA*

Elias Howe
The Man Who Changed The World
No1 New Release Amazon Oct 2019.

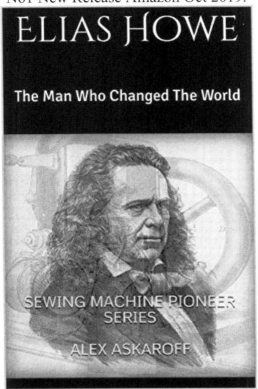

Anyone who uses a sewing machine today has one person to thank, Elias Howe. He was the young farmer with a weak body who figured it out. Elias's life was short and hard, from the largest court cases in legal history to his adventures in the American Civil War. He carved out a name that will live forever. Elias was 48 when he died. In that short time he really was the man who changed the world.

Printed in Great Britain
by Amazon

54873117R00029